To Ron,
prayers and deepest support
from my heart!

James D. Kix Freeman
May 29, 2001

MW01166560

Love
Is Strong
as Death

Also by James Dillet Freeman

Books:

The Case for Reincarnation

The Hilltop Heart: Reflections of a Practical Mystic

Of Time and Eternity

Once Upon a Christmas

Prayer: The Master Key

The Story of Unity

What God Is Like

Cassettes:

Angels Sing in Me: The Best of James Dillet Freeman

Freeman's Christmas Stories

Moving Through Grief

Love
Is Strong as Death

James Dillet Freeman

With an Introduction by
Philip White

Unity
House

Unity Village, Missouri

First Edition 2000

Copyright © 2000 by James Dillet Freeman. All rights reserved. No part of this book may be used or reproduced in any manner whatsoever without written permission from Unity House except in the case of brief quotations embodied in critical articles and reviews or in the newsletters and lesson plans of licensed Unity teachers and ministers. For information, address Unity House, Publishers, Unity School of Christianity, 1901 NW Blue Parkway, Unity Village, MO 64065-0001.

To receive a catalog of all Unity publications (books, cassettes, compact discs, and magazines) or to place an order, call the Customer Service Department: (816) 969-2069 or 1-800-669-0282.

The publisher wishes to acknowledge the editorial work of Michael Maday, Raymond Teague, and Joy Dupont; the copy services of Kay Thomure, Shari Behr, and Deborah Dribben; the production help of Rozanne Devine and Jane Blackwood; and the marketing efforts of Allen Liles, Jenee Meyer, and Sharon Sartin.

Cover design by Gail Ishmael

Cover photo by © Rob Matheson/THE STOCK MARKET

Cover photo of Katherine Freeman and college photo of author from James Dillet Freeman collection

Photo of James Dillet Freeman by Gene King/Unity Photography

Photo of the weeping angel, Scottsville, Texas, by Sylvia Teague

Interior design and composition by Coleridge Design

Library of Congress Cataloging-in-Publication Data
Freeman, James Dillet.
    Love is strong as death / James Dillet Freeman ; with an introduction by Philip White. — 1st cd.
        p.   cm.
    ISBN 0-87159-246-0 (softcover)
    1. Love poetry, American.   2. Married people Poetry.
3. Spouses—Death Poetry.   4. Grief Poetry.   I. Title.
PS3556.R388L58   2000
811'.54—dc21   99-16621
                                                                        CIP

Canada BN 13252 9033 RT

Unity House feels a sacred trust to be a healing presence in the world. By printing with biodegradable soybean ink on recycled paper, we believe we are doing our part to be wise stewards of our Earth's resources.

"Set me as a seal upon your heart,
as a seal upon your arm;
for love is strong as death,
passion fierce as the grave.
Its flashes are flashes of fire,
a raging flame.
Many waters cannot quench love,
neither can floods drown it."

—Song of Solomon 8:6-7 (NRSV)

Contents

Contents

Contents

Part Five
The Shadow Falls
83

Part Six
The Ceremonies
105

Contents

Part Seven
A Time to Mourn
115

Part Eight
Love Is Strong as Death
131

Introduction

"Where there is sorrow, there is holy ground."
—Oscar Wilde

There is a small room at the top of a narrow staircase in an old farmhouse in Lee's Summit, Missouri. It is a comfortable room encircled with small bookcases, several overstuffed chairs, and a desk with a typewriter next to the window. Here the poet and author James Dillet Freeman, for a good part of his sixty-year literary career, has poured out words of faith and love to hundreds of thousands of readers who love his writing. The room's windows, which face south and east, once overlooked farm fields. But, as it always does, life's changes have worked their magic and now the windows frame huge maple and elm trees that have grown up over the years. No longer does the house stand alone along a gravel country road, but nestles together with others along a tree-lined paved lane.

One day several years ago, Jim asked me to come by and read a manuscript he was thinking of submitting to a publisher. As I mounted the staircase and settled into a chair in that small room, I was not prepared for the human depth of the story I was about to read nor the power of the words which told it. They were words of loss and of grief and of love.

The details are simple enough. In 1934 James Freeman married Lucy Katherine Veronica Gilwee. They lived and worked in Kansas City for Unity School of Christianity. Then in 1947 Katherine became ill and was diagnosed with an advanced malignancy. After ten months of decline, she passed away in September 1948.

Such plain facts are enough for the daily news. In a culture increasingly uncomfortable with the untidy nature of bereavement and grief, our public forum is content with a soulless presentation. And when grief goes on too long, our discomfort level rises and patience grows short: "Isn't it time for John to be over it by now?"

Most of us will experience the death of one we love. From that moment forward our lives will be changed. We may continue doing the same things we did before, but if we are like most people, when the presence of those who trod with us along the path of everyday living has passed beyond our sight, the path we trod together no longer glows with the same promise and joy. We deal with feelings of emptiness and hopelessness, but the rest of the world goes on quite well around us. Our tradition keeps grief sequestered, getting us through it before anyone knows we've had it. And the soul of our loss goes incognito through the public square.

Then what we show to the world often looks like a minor disappointment, an upset to our plans, a simple adjustment in the details of our lives—perhaps some new tires, a tune-up, a little time, and we're on our way again. In the process, grief's purpose goes unexplored and is obscured.

So grief in our culture is a discrete suffering. I'm sure that's why poets walked the earth in earlier times, why bards came suddenly upon the town square and, by their words, released joy and love, and set grief free in those who gathered there. For the spirit of the poet is revelatory. And the poet's art has the power to open doors of the heart that have been bolted closed.

That's what I discovered as I turned the pages of Jim's manuscript on that afternoon. The soul of the story came flowing forth. Holy ground appeared. Jim, I realized, had taken seriously Longfellow's great insight: "There is no grief like the grief that does not speak." Here was grief liberated from silence. Here was love's heartache set free in language and then submitted openly to life to be transformed. Here were the honest passions of heart and mind that form the starting point of our conversation with eternity. Here were haunting reflections of the extremes of human consciousness—from the heavenly heights of love to the depths of hellish torments and despair. "These poems," wrote Jim, "are the tears I kept."

The Mending Spirit

In every relationship is a spirit of mending. It is one of the great powers of human nurture and of the spirit. We hold our love for another in our hearts and nurture that love in the circle of our relationship. Within this circle of love, what needs fixing, we fix. We repaint the house and repair the broken gutter. When conflict comes, we apologize and bring flowers. Skinned knees get bandages, and our bodies even repair themselves throughout our lives. We have a mending spirit—mending is our "thing."

But then we come face-to-face with what we cannot fix. The death of the other we cannot fix. And so in death the mending spirit seems helpless. "When she died," Jim wrote, "my first thought was to run away. The house was so full of her."

Yet he did not run away. Instead, he did what it was uniquely his to do. He put pen to paper and wrote it all down. He wrote it from his heart as he experienced his wife Katherine's illness and death. And in his writing, the mending spirit returns—throwing off its helplessness, seeking a larger circle of love, and discovering death's own limitation.

In Katherine, Jim saw the faith he knew he wanted. In her response to her illness, she became his teacher. His faith, he said, "was fugitive," in comparison to hers. "My faith," he wrote, "was no more than an infant's cry, hoping to whine its way out of the pain; She saw life in a larger frame than I, saw us against eternity." Much to his admiration, her vision transcended their horizon. "She knew Something I could but hope at, she saw clear Something I felt but dimly to be true; I stood as far away, but she stood near."

"How could she be afraid to die, she said; To fear death was as foolish as to be afraid on Monday to get out of bed and go to work. On Monday morning she would rise and go to work, and that was all."

And so the mending spirit worked in him to gradually enlarge the circle created by his relationship with Katherine. "We must go forward on faith," he wrote, "for this I know, that faith is life and prayer is life. I learned it from my dying wife."

Love's Larger Circle

More than anything, it was a love story that passed through my hands that afternoon. From an experience that would ordinarily narrow our heart's capacity came a vision of Love's larger circle—a circle that, in the end, reveals death's weakness. The mending spirit, unable to fix death, takes hold of Jim's writing to bring expression to both the honest pain of grief and the blossoming of transcendent love.

Some might not think so. There will be those who will turn away in shock from some of what these poems hold. For in the midst of pain and suffering, what do fear and cynicism and anger toward God and others have to do with love? But if life is calling us all to expand our soul's circumference, will there not be stress? When love enlarges, will there not be a fracturing of the margins of our territory? For the tree to shade more weary travelers, the bark must crack and split. Like continents moving on earth's surface is the gradual widening of Love's circle in us. There are stress fractures and fault lines and the flow of molten rock.

Remember, until the Nazarene called for a wider circle of love, they came to stone the woman taken in adultery. And they broke out the fire hoses and dogs in Selma, Alabama, when love's perimeter surged forward. Could it be that pain and love go hand in hand—that pain is part of love's slow annexation of our being? Jim writes:

> For the soul takes its highest gain
> Not from love's pleasure but love's pain,
> And who for love's sake dares the hard
> Hill road finds heaven close and starred.

Goethe once said, "Where there is much light, the shadow is deep." And Saadi observed, "The rose and the thorn, and sorrow and gladness are linked together."

The power of this truth swept over me. Could this be the understanding we need to make sense of pain and anger and even violence wherever we find it?

> I do not understand why this should be,
> But out of pain joy comes and certainty
> From doubt. You cannot waken hell without
> Bestirring heaven; but let demons out,
> And you start flights of angels. This is so,
> Although why it should be I do not know.

In the end it is death's failure that stands out. It is death's limitation that stands revealed. Death may take away the circle that once was our love, but it cannot re-move Love's larger circle into which it must finally be drawn.

> Pain may torment this finity of flesh
> And death may turn this quick to quiet dust.
> Yet death cannot make love's perfection less;
> Pain cannot alter love's unchanging trust
> That there is meaning where no meanings
>   show
> And purpose though no purposes shine
>   through,
> That life and death are but the ebb and flow
> Of being toward the beautiful and true. . . .

> So great is love that but by loving we
> Turn death's defeat into love's victory.

With the reading of the last poem, I put the manu-script down and turned to look out the window to the east. For just a moment my imagination turned back time. The farm fields, long gone, came back into view, and the paved lane became dusty gravel. The trees became young saplings. The homes disappeared as the farmhouse once again stood alone along the road. Could Love's larger circle be like that, I thought, where gradually but relentlessly life fills in the gaps, creating structures which connect us more closely together, building homes, paving roads, showing us the physical connections, calling us to the spiritual connections between us? Is this, in fact, "the ebb and flow of being toward the beautiful and true." Are these the everyday structures of Love's larger circle? And could any of this happen without the heartache of loss? If loss is change, then grief has come often to those who lived in this small farmhouse. Grief accompanies the widening of Love's circle. Ask anyone whose small town is becoming a city.

My prayer is that you will sense the power of the mending Spirit in these writings and when loss comes let this Spirit lead you gently into Love's larger circle. The acceptance of the death of a loved one changes everything. We will either grow bitter at life's pain, or we will love. And I suspect that those who have passed on before us would be the first to rejoice at the widening of Love's circle in us. So that in the end, says the poet:

> Love will rise weeping from its knees
> And raise a world beyond the reach of doom,
> That will survive even our unbelief.

Philip White
January 1999

Editor of *Unity Magazine*, Philip White is an ordained Unity minister who holds a master of divinity degree from St. Paul School of Theology.

His more than thirty years of service at Unity School of Christianity include serving as dean of education for Unity School for Religious Studies and as director of Unity's Continuing Education Program.

These Poems
Are the Tears I Kept

If I am being weak when I feel sad
Remembering my wife and how she died
And how she lived and all the joy we had
Since the loved night when I lay down beside
Her for the first time, and she was my wife
And I her husband, and we were in love
With one another and in love with life;
If to be strong is never to think of
The love I had but cannot have again,
Or when I think of it to feel no pain;
If tears are weakness and not meant for men—
Then I am weak, for often I have lain
Awake and thought about my wife and wept
For her. These poems are the tears I kept.

Part One

*H*earing the Words

1

The doctor said my wife would die.
I only stood; I did not cry;
I put my hand against the wall
To catch myself, but did not fall.

I wondered why he had to shout;
Perhaps the words would not come out,
But every word he spoke was like
A hammer, and I felt it strike.

I could not bear it with my brain;
My body had to take the pain,
And still the ache goes on and on—
I think it never will be gone.

2

My first impulse was toward the telephone.
I had to find someone that I could tell,
It was too much for me to bear alone;
Even the damned inhabitants of hell
Are not forbidden speech with one another.
Struck down and all our grown-up powers undone
We are a small boy crying for his mother;
I had to find someone I loved, someone
Who loved me, and like fiery drops of lead
Spill out the words my heart could not contain
Unspoken. The heart breaks that leaves unsaid
Sorrow too great for silence, breaks with pain.
My call went through. Someone I loved was there,
I seized her voice and gulped it in like air.

3

When pain grows too intense
There comes as now to me
A strange and blessed sense
Of unreality.
I walk through days of daze
I hear as far away,
I see as through a haze,
I watch as at a play,
I read as in a book,
I am a passerby,
I only stand and look
As in a dream where I
Am not but only seem
And like a drunkard, reel
Unfeeling through a dream
Of pain too full to feel.

4

Two weeks before on Sunday afternoon
I had been lying idly on the floor
In tune with all things and all things in tune
With me, it seemed, and wishing nothing more
To make complete my soul's tranquillity,
When my wife walked into the room and said
Quietly, "I am sick," and instantly
Something inside of me went sick with dread.
There was no reason I should feel such fear;
She had been ill before and I had not
Had such a feeling; she did not appear
To be in danger; still through me one thought
Stabbed—and I could not understand it then—
"I shall not ever be happy again!"

Yet as I staggered now through the nightmare
Of the hospital hall toward my wife's room
Where she lay still asleep and unaware
That she must waken to a lingering doom;
And thought how sudden death would be more
    kind
Than the long agony ahead of her;

And was afraid that I might lose my mind
Or might not have the strength of character
To help her in her need—once more to me
Upon the broken record of my pain
The thought returned, "I shall not ever be
Happy again," and there was in my brain
The same sick panic, only now I knew
The reason. It was true, oh, it was true.

5

Feeling the hellish store
Of pain that lay before
Her, through and through me came
Fear like a licking flame.
I cried, O Christ, I cried,
I cried, I cried inside,
And inwardly I said,
Would God we both were dead!

Feeling that I must break,
Not seeing for her sake
That I would have the strength
To go the whole sad length,
I felt I could not bear
To see her, would not dare
To speak lest I should cry
Out that she had to die.

Yet even as I stayed
Outside her room afraid,
I heard as from hell's rim
Her voice cry out, "Jim! Jim!"
Before the sound had died
I bent down at her side,
And so great is love's guile
I met her with a smile.

6

How slow tears are to start!
Some griefs dry up the eyes
And seal the springs of the heart
So that no tears can rise.

But when at last the storm
In the heart's silent deeps
Starts suddenly to form,
Like a vast wind it sweeps—

Sobbing and wild and black
With bursts of tears like hail
To rip the heart and rack
The flesh as with a flail.

It passes and is still.
The heart in anguish then
Lies spent and waiting till
The fury breaks again.

7

I lay upon my bed and could not sleep.
I tried but found I had no power to keep
My mind at saying prayers or counting sheep
As I lay on my bed. I could not sleep;
It seemed to me the more my mind insisted
That flesh lie still, the more my flesh resisted;
I twisted, turned and twisted, turned and twisted,
But could not sleep. Upon my bed I lay
And tried to pray, but when I tried to pray
The thoughts came that I wished to keep away.
I could not sleep as on my bed I lay,
So rose and paced the roaring room awhile,
Then lay back down and tossed another mile
While fear scraped at my reason like a file.
I lay but could not sleep, for round my bed
Came swarms of thoughts that circled in my head
Like damned souls that would not be comforted.
I could not sleep but lay upon my bed
And heard the small night sounds too slight to hear
That did not fall upon my listening ear
But on the quivering and taut of fear

As I lay on my bed and could not sleep,
My thoughts, limbs, bedclothes tangled in a heap,
Waiting time's slow, interminable creep.
I lay upon my bed and could not sleep.

8

My wife was not to be deceived for long.
From the beginning she felt more was wrong
With her than she was told, but feared for me
To know it. I was brave for her and she
Was brave for me. The doctor tried his best
Not to tell her, but she gave him no rest
Until at last he told her. I was loath,
But when she had been told was glad we both
Knew. For we had shared thirteen years with all
The great events that moved the world and small
Heart-hidden incidents that made our life
And linked our separate souls as man and wife:
We had thirsted and from the same cup slaked
Our thirst; fallen asleep together, waked
Together in the morning and at night;
Shared sunlight, moonlight, firelight, candlelight,
And love-light, hope and disappointment, peace
And pain; quarreled and found how quarrels cease
In love's embrace; talked, feared, planned,
    and worked out
Our plans or saw them fail; grew up through doubt
Of one another to love's certainty,
Till I was part and heart of her and she
Of me—one flesh, one mind, one spirit, one!

After such joy together, should we shun
Suffering together? Should we be denied
The right to walk this last mile side by side?
Hell would not be so hard to journey through
If we went hand in hand. The night she knew,
I dreaded going to her, but I went.
I have not ever hurt like that, heart spent
From hurting. But as we lay side by side
And told each other of our love and tried
To keep each other's spirits up, a change
Came over that small room; and this was strange
Because the pain kept on, but through the pain
Something began to shape, and it grew plain
Though it was nothing palpable or gross
To touch but with the heart. We lay close, close
To one another, and an angel came
To us and with its wings put out the flame
And caught us up from hell and wrapped us round

With a wild tenderness I have not found
Again. We clung close as to love's own breast,
Love's heart, and in our torment were at rest.
I do not understand why this should be,
But out of pain joy comes and certainty
From doubt. You cannot waken hell without
Bestirring heaven; but let demons out,
And you start flights of angels. This is so,
Although why it should be I do not know:
The heart must flinch feeling the flames mount
    higher,
But they may be as a refiner's fire.
Those who were soldiers know how keenly then
They felt and lived. Men find their greatness when
Life lays the greatest tasks on them. Before
Impossibles the soul may fail yet soar!

They who have not known what it is to share
Sorrow and pain beyond their strength to bear,
Who never have been swept too far from land
By the sea's fury, may not understand:
I pity them, their soul is incomplete,
Who never faced the storm or felt defeat.
Soul, are you in the deeps? It is all right;
They shall but be the measure of your height.

9

I hovered near her, quick to note
Each turn, fear bounding at my throat;
And every sign however small
And signs that were not signs at all
But empty fears I magnified
A thousandfold; and though I tried
To hide my fears from her, she caught
The secret impulse of my thought
And felt for me, tossed without rest
Between the hollow and the crest
Of hopelessness and hope. The shock
Of the storm smote her, but the rock
Of her calm spirit stood untouched.
Out of my hopeless hope I clutched

At her serene simplicity,
But what she had eluded me.
She had the small child's gift to live
But one day at a time and give
Its undivided self to each
Moment that flies. I had to reach
Forever for tomorrow's pain,
Used up my present strength to strain
At future fears, and could not say
With her, I am alive today.
She faced the fact, then let it go
And lived as if she did not know,
Lived each day as it came, and she
Had strength to bear eternity.

Part Two

The Same World—
Yet No Longer the Same

10

Before we had discovered she was ill
We had been looking at fur coats, so I
Made up my mind that she would have one still
For Christmas, though I knew that she might die
And never get to wear it. We did not
Have too much money saved, and we might need
It all for some important use; forethought
Said I was foolish, but I paid no heed.
Sometimes to be a loving fool is wise—
And who wants wisdom on a Christmas morn?
I knew the coat would be a grand surprise
And did not care if it was ever worn.

On Christmas morning I was up at dawn
And lit the tree as I had all my life;
And then by candlelight with carols on
The record player I led in my wife,
And we sat down together on the floor
And opened up our presents one by one
And oh-ed and ah-ed at everything and swore
That Christmas never had been so much fun;

Though I was grateful that the room was dark.
For if my eyes held tears, the darkness kept
Her from discovering them; she could not mark
My tears if I kept smiling while I wept.
Then, after we had opened everything
In sight and I had piled up the debris
Of paper, boxes, ribbons, wrappings, string,
I brought the fur coat to her. Tremblingly,
She took it in her hands and stood and tried
It on. Oh, she looked beautiful in it!
Then for a moment we stood side by side,
And I could see her face and it was lit
With the still tears of love she would not shed
And the still joy of love she could not tell.
And for a moment not a word was said,
But there we stood and there we kissed in hell.

11

My wife and I stayed home on New Year's Eve.
Though several of our friends had asked us out
To New Year's parties, I did not believe
That she was strong enough to be about.

There was a blizzard howling in the street,
But we were not concerned about the weather:
The bitter music of the wind and sleet
Half-heard but made us feel closer together.

I held her close and wished for nothing more.
I was just happy to have her to touch
And talk to. Sitting quietly before
The fire, we did not even talk of much.

I only wished to hold her close to me
And waited for the new year to begin—
And tried my hardest not to know that she
Would never see another new year in.

12

My wife was not content to lie in bed.
"This will be like a passing dream," she said.
As soon as she was able she was out
Of bed as if she did not have a doubt,
Working around the house, trying to cook
The meals she thought I needed, trying to look
After my needs, and I could hear once more
The tip-tap of her feet upon the floor.
I think that I would recognize that sound
If I heard it in heaven and turn round
And look for her dear face. She had a way
Of walking that was music, quick and gay.
I listened for the sound as for a song
I knew by heart. But it did not last long.
Slowly her steps grew slower. She might hide
Her weakness from my eyes, and this she tried
As long as she was able, but death beat
Out his dark message with her faltering feet.

13

One evening—she had then been sick about
A month—Katherine would not come eat with me.
I grew alarmed when she did not get out
Of bed. "Are you in pain?" I asked, but she
Lay silent with her face turned toward the wall.
After a while she said, "I am all right,
Just feeling sorry for myself is all."
I tried to think of some way that I might
Be of some comfort to her, but when I
Thought to lie down by her, she drew away.
"Please go away," she said. "I have to try
To work this out inside myself." She lay
Alone perhaps an hour or two, and then
Rose and we did not speak of it again.

14

There was so little I could do;
There was so much I wanted to.
I would have felt that I was blest
Could I have waited all the rest
Of my life on her, heart and hand.
This Katherine would not understand
And worried lest she might become
Helplessly ill and burdensome.
"You can't do woman's work," she said,
But I could cook and make her bed
And hold her when she hurt and run
Errands for her. What could be done
I loved to do, grateful for all
Love's chores, and finding them too small.

Love does not labor as for hire
And hoard its strength lest it should tire
And haggle over terms of pay
And hours. Love gives itself away,
Seeking not for its own but for
Ways that it may be giving more,

Knowing that he who bears love's cross
And servitude suffers no loss,
For the soul takes its highest gain
Not from love's pleasure but love's pain,
And who for love's sake dares the hard
Hill road finds heaven close and starred.

15

I have but one small angel, Lord.
She is so small she cannot be
Too high in heaven's hierarchy.
You who have many can afford
To let her stay awhile with me.

You have tall crowds of seraphim
To sing "Te Deum." Out of all
Heaven you will not miss one small
Angel in canticle and hymn,
Who had the farthest choir stall.

But I would miss her more than life,
More than I have the skill to tell,
This angel who left heaven to dwell
In love with me and be my wife
And make a heaven of my heart's hell.

16

I wish that I could keep
The gift I wrung from hell
And had grief's skill to tell
The shallows from the deep,
And power to separate
From living's much ado
The beautiful and true.

I stood before death's gate
And saw things at their worth.
How mean and meaningless
Is all the petty press
Of fears that sweep the earth—
The hates with which men burn,
Fame's noise, ambition's strain,
The game of loss and gain,
Which is life's chief concern.

The pride and pomp of life
I weighed as on a scale;
It weighed less than the frail
Spring flower form of my wife.

What clear sight weeping brings!
I saw beside my love
The unimportance of
All unimportant things.

17

On the first day that felt like spring
I took my wife out for a ride;
We looked and looked at everything.
But everything was black inside
My mind, for I kept thinking then
That I would come this way again
But she would not be at my side.
I turned away my face to hide
What I was thinking, but she caught
My inward state, though I denied
That I had such a gloomy thought.
Softly she said, "We are alive
Today and going for a drive."
But even though I knew I ought
To show more joy, my gloom crept back
And all the thoughts I had were black.

18

If I had never loved you,
If I had never lain
Heart hearing heart beside you,
I would not have this pain.

I would not have this sorrow,
I would not have this pain,
But if I had not loved you,
I would have lived in vain.

Part Three

Contending With God

19

When I saw my wife suffer, I cursed God.
I damned whatever made the world and me—
Why was it not content to leave the clod
A clod, why fire it for such agony?
But sometimes I would kneel and scrape and whine
For pity in the world's unpitying ears;
It was not moved by any plea of mine—
My curses or my coaxing or my tears.
The hell was to be helpless. Even to crawl
Was better. Christ, for something I could hate
And smash! There was not anything at all
But wait and watch and wait and watch and wait.
Hell must have agonies, but after earth's
I do not think that they shall hurt us worse.

Seeing me kneel she wept for me, but smiled
To hear me curse. She said God understood
That I was not grown-up but still a child
That could not stand, caught handholds where
   I could,
Tumbling at the first push of doubt. She knew
Something I could but hope at, she saw clear
Something I felt but dimly to be true;
I stood as far away, but she stood near.

Love Is Strong as Death
This was not faith she had, but something more;
What she knew, she knew as I know my hand
And as I know that two and two makes four:
You had to know my wife to understand.
She was not stumbling as I stumbled blind,
But God had told her what was on His mind.

How could she be afraid to die, she said;
To fear death was as foolish as to be
Afraid on Monday to get out of bed
And go to work. On Monday morning she
Would rise and go to work, and that was all.
I know, she said. And somehow when you heard
Her say it, you knew too. The lurking small
Uncertainties dispelled at her soft word.
You knew the moment that you looked at her
She would meet death like life, her shoulder out
To take the weight. It was in character.
Not even the capacity for doubt
Was in her. She believed that all is well;
It did not shake her faith to wake in hell.

20

My faith was no more than an infant's cry,
Hoping to whine its way out of the pain;
She saw life in a larger frame than I,
Saw us against eternity, saw plain—
Not with the mind, but feeling with the heart.
She did not want the pain, but she could see
That being what we are is still part
Of the soul's reaching for infinity.
Her faith was a deep river, a still flowing;
Her soul in secret met her secret lord
In a communion not of words, a knowing
Deeper than thought, and they were in accord.
Pain's broken edges cut her, but she stood
Unchanged. Hell has no power to harm the good.

What can fear do to him who has no fears?
Storms cannot keep the river from the sea;
A quiet heart through life's unquiet years
Flows like a river of eternity.
Pain may torment this finity of flesh
And death may turn this quick to quiet dust.
Yet death cannot make love's perfection less;
Pain cannot alter love's unchanging trust
That there is meaning where no meanings show

And purpose though no purposes shine through,
That life and death are but the ebb and flow
Of being toward the beautiful and true.
Having seen faith where only fear should be,
Through doubt I can reach blind for certainty.

21

The heart has a sure touchstone which is love
To try all other truths if they be true.
Love's truth is truer than the part-truths of
The mind. It was this lover's truth she knew,
Her certainty in life's uncertain land,
Tearing the darkness as birth tears the caul,
A truth that only heart can understand
How love has made the world in spite of all.
Even in death it showed her all is well
And love's frail tremulous bright star may rise
And burn in beauty even over hell—
I saw this dimly as before sunrise.
So great is love that but by loving we
Turn death's defeat into love's victory.

22

I took up golf. I had to have something
To do at times, and I could walk around
The links and be outdoors when it was spring.
I was no good at golf, but I could pound
The ball, and when I missed it I could swear—
Swear at myself, at God, at the unkind
Fates that I put the blame on, till the air
Was blue. It helped me keep my peace of mind.
My instinct warned me that I did not dare
To think of what was happening to my wife
Or I would lose my power to stand and bear,
And yet I had to vent my rage at life.
Out on the golf course a missed putt could be
In miniature the whole of tragedy.

23

Often I prayed. To bear the pain
Of my beloved and stay sane
I had to pray. I could not find
Much meaning reaching with my mind,
Though I would rack my brain and think
Sometimes to reason's farthest brink;
But where thought ended, there I made
A stride into the dark, and prayed.

What was there I would not have tried
For her I loved? Swallowing pride
And struggling with agnostic doubt,
In many a church I sought God out
And prayed for faith I often felt
Had been denied me. Long I knelt
To God and saint to catch a trace
Of pity on their plaster face.

It might be that I did not pray
Aright. I taught my tongue to say,
"God's will be done," but my heart cried

Only, "I want my wife." I lied
If I said any other prayer.
That one was all I meant. If there
Was God, was He less kind than I?
Could Life will that the living die?

Why should she die who was the best
Person I knew, the loveliest,
Noblest, gentlest, kindest of
Women, too young for death, in love
With me and I in love with her—
When other men on all sides were
Praying that they might lose their wives
And living long and loveless lives?

What I prayed for I did not get.
My mind has not been able yet
To see the reason for the pain—
And still I did not pray in vain.
Whether or not a single word
Of all my prayers was ever heard
I cannot say, but I can see
The difference they made in me.

For where I could not stand
I stood, and kept on feeling for the good
When in my heart I heard the tread
Of the wild horses of my dread,
And where I thought I would come out
Bitter and certain of my doubt,
Strangely instead I came out more
Certain of meaning than before.

24

I cannot think how Love could will
A world of pain and death; and still
My heart keeps saying, "Life's events
Though now they puzzle us make sense."
As infants sob in fear bereft
Of thought and hope when they are left
Alone for a few hours, so we
Are infants of eternity.

We know but little. Our mind fumbles
As with a jigsaw puzzle, stumbles
On a few facts, and piecing these
Together, cries, "Life looks like trees!"
But finding one more piece exclaims
"What seemed like trees is really flames!"
And shall we as we stumble on
See that the flames burst into dawn?

The wisest man can only take
The universe on faith and make
It good or ill according to
His disposition. What is true
Is still beyond us. We must go
Forward on faith, for this I know,
That faith is life and prayer is life.
I learned it from my dying wife.

Still the Glory Is Not Gone

One night I lay down by my wife
So tired that I was tired of life,
So close to love, so close to death
I lay, almost too close for breath.

There from the midnight cliffs of mind,
Leaving all things and thought behind,
I looked at everything on earth
And saw what everything is worth.
I saw then what life's meanings are,
What I am doing on this star,
Citizen of the universe,
Meeting the better and the worse,
Whether willing or whether loath,
For the law of life is the law of growth.
I saw the secret in the seed,
Saw the lily in the weed,
Saw life in death, saw in the tomb
Only the resurrecting womb!
I looked at life and saw it plain,
And saw the meaning of the pain,

Saw heaven's rim though it was hell,
And though I had no words to tell
What I had seen, I understood—
Saw through the pain and saw it good!
And knew that somehow I am part
Of being, heart of the inmost heart!

Then through my hell of helplessness,
I felt an unseen presence press,
And when I rose it lingered on,
And still the glory is not gone.

I Am There

I had gone to pray for Katherine in the Silent Unity prayer room at 917 Tracy in Kansas City. As I sat there in agony, unable to bring my mind into enough order to speak words of prayer, suddenly I heard a voice. The voice was so real, so audible that I looked around to see who was there. The voice said, "Do you need Me? I am there." As I sat there, the voice continued.

Do you need Me?
I am there.
You cannot see Me, yet I am the light you see by.
You cannot hear Me, yet I speak through your
    voice.
You cannot feel Me, yet I am the power at work in
    your hands.
I am at work, though you do not understand My
    ways.
I am at work, though you do not recognize My
    works.
I am not strange visions. I am not mysteries.
Only in absolute stillness, beyond self, can you know
    Me as I am, and then but as a feeling and a faith.
Yet I am there. Yet I hear. Yet I answer.
When you need Me, I am there.
Even if you deny Me, I am there.

Even when you feel most alone, I am there.

Even in your fears, I am there.

Even in your pain, I am there.

I am there when you pray and when you do not
    pray.

I am in you, and you are in Me.

Only in your mind can you feel separate from Me,
    for only in your mind are the mists of "yours"
    and "mine."

Yet only with your mind can you know Me and
    experience Me.

Empty your heart of empty fears.

When you get yourself out of the way, I am there.

You can of yourself do nothing, but I can do all.

And I am in all.

Though you may not see the good, good is there, for
    I am there.

I am there because I have to be, because I am.

Only in Me does the world have meaning; only out
    of Me does the world take form; only because of
    Me does the world go forward.

I am the law on which the movement of the stars
    and the growth of living cells are founded.

I am the love that is the law's fulfilling.

I am assurance.

I am peace.

I am oneness.

I am the law that you can live by.

I am the love that you can cling to.

I am your assurance.

I am your peace.

I am one with you.

I am.

Though you fail to find Me, I do not fail you.

Though your faith in Me is unsure, My faith in you
    never wavers, because I know you, because
    I love you.

Beloved, I am there.

Part Four

The Struggle With Others

25

I overheard friends talking. One was saying
That she felt sorry for my wife and me,
But looking at her empty life and weighing
Her soul against our pain and jeopardy,
I thought, My pity is for you, my friend,
Who in a lifetime has not learned to live,
Who has no deeps to which you may descend,
Who never has known what it is to give
Yourself in perilous ecstasy away.
Though for a hundred years you may sail round
The safe, untroubled waters of your bay
While we who have put out to sea have drowned,
Yet for your century with no love in it,
I would not trade my love's least, anguished
    minute.

26

She wanted a new stove. Our old one was
Worn out, she said; it was all rust and flaws
And blacked the pans and caused the cakes to fall.
And all of this was true, and still with all
We had to have, a stove was one thing we
Could do without, I thought, most easily.
She could not cook on it; even the smell
Of food now made her sick; she was not well
Enough to eat, let alone cook. And still
She wanted a new stove with all her will.

There was so much we needed money for.
Her brother who owned an appliance store
Thought it was plain damn foolishness. What could
She want with a new stove? I understood
Faintly, but had no way of telling him;
He thought it was just a sick woman's whim,
And so put off delivery as long
As he was able, but her will was strong,
Stronger than his or mine, and what she felt
Was right was right to the end. Body might melt
Away till it was tenuous as smoke,
But her determination never broke.

She felt that it was right for us to get
A stove; on that her heart and mind were set.
She wanted it not for herself, but me.
A stove to her meant home and family,
Somehow meant hope that after she was gone
The home might stand and I might still go on
Having friends in to dine, making a life
Of sorts. She was trying to be my wife,
Looking after my needs. She knew that I,
Left to my man's devices, would not buy
A stove, not seeing with a woman's eyes.
Still, though at first I had not thought it wise,
I wanted what she wanted; if it were
Foolishness, I would be foolish for her.

I called her brother. He kept promising
The stove in a few days, but did not bring
It. This went on for weeks. Each evening when
I came from work she had me call again
And ask why the stove was not there. Bedfast
Though she was, she would not let go. At last
She brought the struggle to a sudden end.

One evening she informed me that a friend
Who had been visiting her had called another
Store. Now she wanted me to call her brother
And make it plain. I had not ever heard
Her swear before but somehow she was stirred
About that stove. "Tell him to get the hell
Out here tomorrow if he hopes to sell
A stove to us. We'll give him one day more,
Then we will order from the other store.
You call him up and tell him just that way,"
She said. She lay and listened. The next day
The stove was there. As soon as it had come
She made the perilous long journey from
Her bedroom to the kitchen just to look
At it. She knew she would not ever cook
On it. "It's pretty, isn't it?" she said,
And leaning on my arm went back to bed.

27

How can so large a spirit be
Lodged in such small captivity?
The wan medallion of this face,
Thin hands as linen fine as lace,
Body as spirit delicate
As the reflection of sunlit
Ripples, as nothing you will find
Outside a lover's or poet's mind,
A Dresden china shepherdess
Compounded out of selflessness
And faith and the magnificence
Of courage. Not large but intense,
So quietly and subtly glows
Her influence that no one knows
He stands in it, so gently caught
He feels that it was his own thought.

28

How lacking in humanity can be
Those whose profession is humanity!
The doctor would not even make a call.
He had no time, he said, and after all
What could he do except run up a bill?
Although he did not think of this until
My wife had grown so weak she could no longer
Call at his office. When she had been stronger
And he could pocket a quick fee without
Effort, he had shown no concern about
Saving us money. In all, he came twice
And let me know that was a sacrifice.

I felt it might have cheered her had he come,
Taken her pulse, asked questions, prattled some
Doctor's chitchat, she was so long in bed.
But there was nothing he could do, he said,
And so that I would not disturb his slumber
Thoughtfully gave me his assistant's number,
Who proved to be a young man not as bright
But as reluctant to make calls at night.

I did not like the doctor, but I felt
Perhaps his ice was fear lest his heart melt
At life's much sadness. He was harsh to me
To cover up his own futility.
His rudeness sprang not from indifference
But from despair and was his soul's defense.

29

I had not missed a family, having none;
But now I wished we were a part of one,
For I could see there is a kind of strength
In families, in their very breadth and length,
In being kin, in cousin, uncle, brother,
Son, and grandson all bound to one another,
In being part of something that goes on
When you and your green hour of life are gone.

Some vines root everywhere they touch the
    ground.
Uproot one, and the other members, bound
To one another, find a sustenance
Together and grow on in spite of chance.
But she and I were like two vines that shoot
Upward together from a single root
And twining round each other grow apart
From all the rest into each other's heart.
And when she withered, all that had sustained

Me withered and no strength for life remained.
And then I learned what friends are for. They came
And gave themselves to us, and at the flame
Of friendship I could warm my heart and live.

Learning our pain, people were quick to give.
How good most people are! They tried to be
Of help, although sometimes but bumblingly,
And held their hearts out to us and their hands
To ease our pain. We could not make demands
On those who gave. They only gave because
They wanted to, gave not to win applause
For giving or to flatter or to make
Money, but gave from goodness, for love's sake
Only. Our helplessness had power to reach
Through walls that force and fortune could not
    breach.

And we found no small person's gift too small.
I learned to value friends, grateful for all
Proffers of help. Where once I might have spurned
A hand stretched out in friendship, now I turned

Eagerly to grasp hold of it. We can
Proudly put on the self-sufficient man
When life runs in the shallows, but swept out
Beyond our depth, our strength unstrung, in doubt
Even as to the worth of life, we clutch
At any loving thought, at love's least touch.

30

There is no substitute for love. The day
Came when I had to find someone to stay
With Katherine and take care of her, and I
Found that a loving heart is hard to buy.
I looked into hard faces, listened to
Coarse voices asking what they had to do,
Showing concern only for their own ease,
Only indifference. Not to such as these
Would she be the beloved, and I could
Not leave her with them, for I knew she would
Make few demands on them. I hoped to find
Someone who looked as if she might be kind,
Clean and soft-spoken, with a gentleness
About her motions, who would neither press
Attention on my wife nor overlook
Her needs. My wife wanted one who could cook
For me. She was afraid that I was being
Neglected since she was no longer seeing
After my needs. I searched and searched, and in
The end I hired someone who had not been
A nurse before, but showed love's reticence
And looked as if she might have common sense.

I preferred some slight awkwardness like hers
To skill with clinical thermometers
And nothing more. Later I had to hire
Practical nurses too. Their one desire
Seemed to be to take Katherine's temperature.
It would have been more than I could endure
To have those bungling fools pestering me
With such nonsense outside eternity.
But Katherine smiled at them. They seemed to need
To do it, she said. To know how to read
Thermometers was probably their chief
Accomplishment, and she could stand the brief
Discomfort of it rather than upset
The routine they depended on. She let
Them stick thermometers in her and smiled
At them as at the antics of a child.

I swore, but nurses were so hard to get that
I put up with them—even with Violet.
My wife liked her, feeling secure in her
Cradle-like hands and country character.
But she took the sharp edge of my wife's pain
And drove it like a knife into my brain.
Each evening she would wait for me to tell

Me how my wife felt, paint the pain so well,
In such detail dissect each ghastly feeling
That she would send me sweating, stumbling,
    reeling.
Instead of words I wished she had a quirt
To whip me with. I was quick to the hurt
My wife had, felt it deeply with my soul
And keenly with my senses, with the whole
Of my devotion, with my hopes and fears,
With all our life together, all the years
We had spent side by side—one heart, one flesh,
One feeling. Having been one happiness,
Now we were one anguish. What could she feel
That I did not feel too? Pain was the seal
Of our communion. Joys and pangs of sense

And spirit linked us ever in intense
Inseparable oneness. If she felt
Pain I too felt it, needed no hell's pelt
Of words to make me feel it. With all of
My power to feel I felt it, with my love!
I hurt enough, I did not need that hag
To twist my brain and wring it like a rag.

31

A few who came for love's sake tried too hard
At times, and by their too much giving marred
The gift. For some, seeing me downcast, cried:
Cheer up! Cheer up! Did they not think I tried?
Sometimes I swore at them. Not to be rude
Is grief's most difficult beatitude.
I was cheerful for her, cheerful as I
Could be, that is; for sometimes I would cry
When I was with her, but she understood
That I might want to cry, and felt it good.
She would have thought I was a lunatic
Had I been cheerful when she was so sick.

Still others thought they had to sympathize.
But seeing tears well up in other eyes,
I could not hold the dikes of my own soul,
And though I struggled hard for self-control,
The flood rose in me then. I could not keep
My own grief back when I saw others weep.
All that I could do then was turn and flee.

I did not look either for sympathy
Or cheering up. They helped me most who were
Themselves and did what they could do for her
And me because they loved us, wished to share
Our loneliness made not too hard to bear
By being shared. It was not what they brought—
Some easy gift of words or depth of thought—
It was not anything they did or said.
It was just standing by me in my dread,
Being there when I needed them. How small
And mean we may look when life makes no call
On us for more, but when the need comes through,
Then we discover deeps we never knew
In one another. The unlikeliest
Sometimes can reach a hand up to the best.
Around the lonely islands of men's souls
An infinite estranging ocean rolls,
Yet deeper than the separating sea
There runs through all mankind a unity
We can but sense, for no one comprehends
How it may be, but lovers know, and friends.

32

I have been baptized in the flood
Of Phlegethon burst out of hell;
It hisses in my veins, not blood;
I drink of it as from a well.

This is the baptism of life
That water is no symbol of,
But fire that folds me like a wife
With agony instead of love.

33

What little things we can be thankful for
When there is nothing to be glad about;
Then we take little and expect no more,
Happy that life has doled its little out.
When we are down, let any small dog think
To wag his tail at us, he cheers us up;
When we are thirsty, we take any drink
And do not look too closely at the cup.
So when the summer turned out cooler than
The oven it had been a year ago,
You would almost have thought the weatherman
And I were brothers and have looked for snow
To hear me rhapsodize about the weather—
And there were scarcely two fine days together!

Part Five

The Shadow Falls

34

As Katherine's life slipped from her, she became
So weak that she could hardly brush her hair.
She thought she looked untidy and would blame
Herself for it. She said it was not fair
To make friends see her when she looked so sick.
Each day she washed and brushed as best she could
And like a banner put on her lipstick.
She had no looking glass. Thinking she would
Want it, I brought her one. Quickly she thrust
The thing away. "I do not want to see
Myself," she said, "for I know what I must
Look like and I don't feel I look like me.
Just let me think of me as I have been."
Then she lay back but not as in defeat,
And so that she could not observe how thin
Her arms were she drew over them the sheet.

35

Others saw the frail body wither and
Seeing the toll pain took could hardly stand
To look. I also was not unaware
Of the change in her, for I had to bear
Her in my arms at last and had to tend
The wasted limbs; yet even at the end
She looked as she had always looked to me.

It made me wonder what it is we see
When we look at each other; for I knew
What she must look like to our friends, but to
Me she was still as she had always been;
When I looked at her I saw Katherine.

What did I see that I should note no flaw?
I cannot tell you what it is I saw.
But what I saw then made me realize
That often we do not see with our eyes
Though we may think we do; we see right through
The form that fools us into what is true
Of one another; with a lover's eye

We see our own beloved. That is why
One may find all perfection in a face
Where the rest of us blindly catch no trace
Of beauty. That is why to me my wife
Looked always as she had looked all our life
Together. I had seen her from the start
Not with my eyes, but only with my heart.

36

One hot night she decided she would go
Into the living room. I hoped that she
Would let me carry her, but she said, No,
She could walk! And she walked. Eternity
Will be no longer for me than that hall;
I watched her totter all its endless length
Of agony in terror lest she fall.
She made it, but she knew what little strength
Was left her. "This is I that cannot walk
Alone," she said, and then she wept. I lay
And held her gently, and we did not talk,
For there was nothing I could think to say.

37

Sometimes I wished I were a lunatic
And lacked the power to comprehend or think,
Seeing her sick and sick and sick and sick.
She could not eat, she could not even drink,
But she would try to suck down a few sips
Of water sometimes as I held her up,
And she would smack her baffled, broken lips
And grasp the glass as if it were the cup
Of God's merciless mercy, in her eyes
The greedy glitter of a thing gone mad;
And I must watch her and must realize
That every licked-up drop would only add
To her distress. I felt that God was kind
When sometimes He would let her lose her mind.

38

I have no clear sense of how long things took.
Time was a top whirling inside my brain
Till I lost track of it. Now when I look
Back, what was days is stretched to months of pain
And what was only minutes seems like days,
For in my memory the anguish seems
To have gone on forever. In a haze
Of dread I stumbled, as men may in dreams
That last a moment live for anxious hours.
In the short, sharp space of a gasp or breath
What a long dream of sorrow may be ours!
Now I can understand how men at death
Can watch a crowded lifetime tumble through
Their brain in one brief shudder of review.

39

I could not bid death come or bid him stay.
I knew that death could not be far away,
But could not think of me without my wife.
I felt I had been married all my life;
If there had been a time when I was not
Married, it was a time that I forgot.
I might have made her angry, made her weep;
She might be in another room asleep;
She might be sad; she might have gone somewhere;
She might be sick as now—still she was there
To come home to, to lie down by at last,
To share pain with and when the pain was past
To make love to and share the happiness,
To wake beside, to touch, to hold, to press,
Not separate like a coat but as much a part
Of me as my own hands or my own heart
Or my most secret thoughts—she knew them all.
The music of her voice, of her footfall
Was as familiar as my pulse or breath.
How could I then even imagine death?
Seeing her pain I wanted her to die,
But clung to her as if by clinging I
Might draw her back from that relentless clutch.
I wanted her, I wanted her so much.

40

She was afraid of pain before it started.
"Don't ask me to be brave but let me cry,"
She said, "for I am weak and woman-hearted,
And when I'm frightened, please don't make me try
To act as if I'm not." I could not tell
Her it was I who would be frightened; I
Said, "If you want to, cry," though my heart fell
At thinking of it, for I could not trust
My strength to stand it. Dante painting hell
Said nothing of the place where lovers must
Witness the torment of the one they love.
Since I had buckled at the lightest gust
Of fear before, how could I have enough
Courage to stand up in the hurricane?
God had not made me out of stoic stuff.

I even feared that I might go insane
And fail her utterly. I did not know
That love has power even over pain
And that through loving her my strength would
    grow.
I could not stand alone, but I could share
The agony and sharing it could go,
Because she needed me, beyond despair

And at the crumbling of my universe
Keep on and do what others could not bear
To do for her. As she grew worse and worse
I learned to weep and never shed a tear,
And I could tend her body like a nurse
Unnerved by nothing: love had cast out fear.
My heart was shaken but my hands were sure,
So I found strength to bear the bitter year.
I hoped past hope that there would be a cure,
And then I hoped the pain would not be much.
I gave these hopes up and could still endure;
For when I could endure no more, the touch
Of her hand gave me courage and I could
Stand, and for want of my steadfastness clutch
At hers and hang upon her hardihood.

For she who had affirmed she was afraid
And would cry out at the first twinge withstood
Pain's wildest fury and was not dismayed.
Even at the end when the pain ran uncurbed
In her and flesh was flame and reason strayed,
Still there was something in her undisturbed.
I think her chief emotion was surprise
That she could hurt so much and be unnerved

So little, and I had to doubt my eyes;
For I saw pain take absolute command
Of flesh and mind, yet her real Self would rise
Serene as it had always been and stand
Outside the pain, almost as if it were
Not she but merely led her by the hand.
Dying could make no difference in her.
Her thought was all for others, all for me,
Not for herself; it was her character
To give; she gave almost instinctively,
Not ever knowing it is hard to give,
Not even knowing she was giving. She
Who by her life had taught me how to live
Now taught me how to die by dying. My
Courage was false; my faith was fugitive.
So when she felt death standing too close by,
She bade me take her to the hospital to die.

41

All along she had hoped to know ahead
Of time when she would die; she did not want
To die at home. She wanted me, she said,
To keep on living there, and it would haunt
My heart remembering, "In this room she died."
Living alone would be enough to daunt
Me without that. She thought that if I tried
To keep on living in the house and keep
Around me things that I had lived beside,
Though sometimes memories might make me
    weep,
Still I would find more peace there for a time
Than if I ran away, and I would sleep
Better in my familiar bed; the chime
Of the old banjo clock in the long night,
Sounding the hours like a recurring rhyme—
If I should wake and miss her, as I might—
Would ring like reassurance in my mind.

So when she came to die, she felt it right
To go to the hospital. Still her kind
And quiet spirit was unchanged, her thought
Given to us who would be left behind.
Her life was failing, and we only caught
Brief glimpses of her now. Yet when she drew
Back to us from the darkness, she still sought
To comfort us. Her sister had come to
The hospital. Now Katherine made me take
Her sister's hand in friendship, for she knew
That I would love her sister for her sake
Though often in the past I had been wroth
With her, as in-laws are. She said: "Please make
Friends with each other, for I would be loath
To feel I left you two in enmity.
You are my family, and I love you both.
You are her brother"—and she looked at me;
"You are his sister"—and she looked at her.
Since that time we have been one family,
And I have loved this sister though we were
Not friends before. Meanwhile the woman in
The next bed, though we tried to make no stir,
Became unnerved at seeing death begin,
For at times Katherine's body would assume

Death's cold rigidity and from her thin
And wasted face the staring eyes of doom
Glittered. This terrorized the woman so
That she had to be moved out of the room.
When Katherine found this out she had me go
Apologize as if she were to blame
Because her death was troublesome and slow.

She made me go and eat when evening came.
"Even though I am dying, nonetheless
You have to eat," she said, "and feel no shame.
You must not ever refuse happiness.
I am part of your happiness and approve
Of it." And all that I could do was press
The hand she stretched toward mine and say, "I love
You." But now life and pain had done their worst;
She slept and did not speak again or move.

O all you sufferers in hell who thirst
And stretch out futile hands for some cool drink,
I have seen even an angel so accurst.
Yet being what she was, she did not shrink
From living or from dying, of a will
To be herself even upon the brink

Of doom. Above the pain I see her still
As at the last I saw her turn to me
And stand up in her heart as on a hill
And lift two fingers up to form a "V"
And wave farewell to me, farewell and victory.

42

There was no lightest sound or stir,
No footfall that I caught
To tell me death had come for her;
She is asleep, I thought.

I watched the labor of her breath
Grow still and still and still;
I touched the kindly hand of death
And only felt the chill.

I felt the torment and the strife
Grow faint, and fade, and cease;
It was the passing of her life—
I only felt the peace.

43

No matter how much you have looked ahead
And thought of death, till you have felt death strike
Someone you love and stood by your own dead,
You cannot understand what it is like.

Nothing has happened; only breath has stopped.
Yet suddenly into this null of death,
This nothingness, the one I love has dropped
And vanished as completely as her breath.

She does not answer when I call her name;
I kiss her on the lips—she is not there;
This is not she although it looks the same
And has her face and eyes and mouth and hair.

I have been many miles from her before
And felt alone, but this is not as then;
She has not risen and gone out a door
That sometime I shall see swing in again.

This is a door I cannot even see
But fumble at as one struck blind, deaf, mute,
And only feel death's cold finality
Incomprehensible but absolute.

44

How far between the first kiss and the last!
I can recall the summer night when I
Kissed Katherine for the first time. I was shy;
We sat upon some cottage steps and passed
Small talk between us idly while I massed
My forces and found courage for the try.
I did not know as I took her in my
Arms that that kiss was linking our lives fast.
Only to kiss her was enough for me!
I did not wonder at what lay ahead;
There was no reason why I should feel dread—
I was in love! I had no power to see
That one day she would lie upon a bed
And I would kiss her, and she would be dead.

45

I wonder why before our friends
We have to play a role and keep
A casual air though the world ends:
Before my friends I could not weep.
But when I went to bathe and I
Had turned the water on and knew
That none could hear me should I cry,
Then like a naked child I threw
Away my pride, the hot tears ran
Into the water, and I cried.
I did not have to play the man—
My love had died, had died, had died.

46

Sometimes I think I do not have much faith
In immortality, but when my wife
Was dying, I looked very close at death,
For I lived closer then to death than life
And saw that death is not an end, but breaks
Contact; it is a severing, a sealing
Off of the avenues by which soul makes
Its way into the world. I had a feeling
Of the communications going down,
Not of extinction but of separation.
Death is a secret, silent, snow-locked town.
Sometimes at night I have tuned in a station
Upon the radio and worked to bring
It in till it comes clear and steady, then
Have had it fade completely; fingering
The dials I try to tune it in again.
But nothing comes, and where the sound arose
For a sweet moment from the nothingness,
I feel the nothingness return and close
Around me closer, feel the silence press
Back like the lowering of a vast curtain.
So now death fell between us, yet somewhere
My love's small steady signal, I was certain,
Was going forth upon death's unknown air.

Love Is Strong as Death

For watching her slip gradually out
Of life I had a kind of inward knowing
That was like sight and left no room for doubt
That death is but withdrawal, an ongoing,
That she whom I had loved, whom I had bared
My heart in love to, talked of love with, kept
Love's silence with, borne love's pain with, and
    shared
Love's joy with, and for loss of whom I wept
Was not this body. This familiar form
That she had made herself visible in
And I had found fair, touchable, and warm—
This was not she and had not ever been.
And so I sensed what it must be to die,
Although I could not follow that dark track:
Her body was a bridge that she crossed by
To me and to the world; now she went back.
Although I did not know where she had gone
Beyond the silent boundaries of doom,
I had no doubt that she I loved lived on;
I was a watcher in an empty room.

Part Six

The Ceremonies

47

The undertaker was not gaunt but fat.
His sales talk oozed from him as from a vat
Of oil. He looked as polished and well-lined
As his own caskets and like them designed
To make one think death is a holiday,
A funeral, a de rigueur display.
How fortunate that I had come to him!
Death as he dealt with it was not the grim
Loneliness numbly stealing over me.
His unplain manner made it plain to see
That he was interested in my dead
Because she helped to pay his overhead.
How sad! Tut, tut! So young to have to die!
As the fond husband I would want to buy
The best of course—he buried the elite—
And it should be something in taste but sweet.
Of funerals he had the most extensive
Selection in the town and most expensive.
On learning that I wanted something plain
And cheap, he could not quite conceal his pain.

48

The first night that my wife was dead
I had to drive myself to bed—
The bed that I had loved to share.
I only made myself lie there
Because I saw nowhere to flee,
For I would take myself with me
If I should try to run away;
So there I turned and tossed till day.
But on the second night I crept
Into the bed again—and slept.

49

Much as she used to be
She lies here to the view;
I look at her and see
The face I knew,
The hair that I loved much,
The mouth I loved to kiss,
The hands whose quiet touch
I miss, I miss.

Friends come and look at her;
How mournfully they peer!
As if it truly were
She who lies here.
This is the selfsame form
But she who was my wife
Was gentle, deep, and warm
As love, as life.

50

The funeral did not make me sad.
The only feeling that I had
Was rage that I lacked strength to say
No to a funeral or to stay
Away from it. When I had tried,
The undertaker had implied
That all our friends would think I lacked
Respect for her, and so I backed
Down, but I still hated the whole
Business. I hated with my soul
The funeral home sweet hell so very
Very it was mortuary.
I hated having people come
And stand and stare as at a dumb
Show, for it only seemed to me
To add to death's indignity;
The ones who cried the loudest were
Those who had done the least for her.
I wanted to rise up and shout,
"Come to your senses or get out!"
I hated it, the needless waste,

The useless torment, and all based
Upon a notion that I knew
With my whole soul to be untrue—
That this was Katherine whom we saw.
For when I noted with what awe
Friends stood around her form, afraid,
While this one whispered, that one prayed,
I knew that all this mummery kept
Alive the falsehood, and I wept
Inside myself with shame that I
Was party to so great a lie.

51

On Katherine's birthdays and as Valentines
It had become a custom that I write
Poems for her to add to her delight.
Painstakingly I printed out the lines
On pretty cards that she kept through the years.
Perhaps she took them out sometimes to read
When she was all alone and felt a need
For them; perhaps they were stained by her tears.

Before she died she asked me that I lay
These poems in the casket by her heart.
She wanted them with her, for they were part
Of our love for each other. To her they
Would sing in death more deeply than a choir,
Though no one else would hear them, for they were
The songs of love I only wrote for her,
So they went with her body to the fire.

52

My wife loved lilacs. Often she had said
That if she lived again she hoped that she
Would be a lilac. So when she was dead
My first thought was to plant a lilac tree
Among her ashes. But I grew afraid,
Knowing the tree would be a symbol of
Katherine to me. If it should ever fade,
It would be as a second death of love.

I had a country friend who had a row
Of lilacs by her house, and there I brought
The dust of my beloved, letting no
One know what I was doing. I had thought
The funeral services somehow would be
The end of pain. I had not counted on
This final fillip to my agony;
And now I felt that all my strength was gone,
So heavy to my heart was the small square
Black box I bore. Yet this last act of grace
Was mine to do for her. And I could bear
To do it if I turned away my face

So that I would not see the ashes fall,
Dear ashes that had been so warm with life,
Dear, dear, dear dust to me. Ah, Christ, this small
Handful of dust and bone, this was my wife.

I had to lie down. A long time I lay
Beside the hedge of lilacs, and a part
Of me will never rise and come away,
For I left there two handfuls of my heart.

Part Seven

A Time to Mourn

53

Nothing is as before.
My pleasures make me sad;
I find in things no more
The savor that they had;
Loved voices and loved faces
Make me but lonelier;
In love's familiar places
I only think of her.

Did I seek a new truth?
It was to her I brought it.
Did I buy a new suit?
It was for her I bought it.
When did I write a word
That was not for my wife?
All that I read or heard
Or hoped or made of life
I gathered up and took
To her, and from the thought
We shared and from the look
We joined, the casual caught

Flame, and our whole life glowed.
And when I needed strength,
From loving strength flowed
To go the trouble's length.

The things I once loved best
Become now hard to bear;
Gone is my golden zest
For life; I do not care
What joy or grief time brings:
She will not come again.
Alone I do the things
We did together then.

54

I wear no mourning for my wife, but wear
My mourning in my heart. If I wore black
I would not love her more or bring her back.
Mourning is not the measure of despair
Or love. I cannot think a thought or speak
A word that has not Katherine in it, cries
Not: Katherine, Katherine, Katherine! Inward lies
My oneness with her. Not in visibles seek
To understand how she has grown a part
Of me and is my faith in joy and life.
If you would know my feeling for my wife,
Listen to the impulses of my heart:
Her unheard music only can be caught
In my soul's silences and springs of thought.

55

If tears would wear away the rocks
The mountains would be in the sea.
So many are the aches and shocks
Besetting our humanity.

But mountains are unmoved by grief
Or anything, and rocks are gray
Forever. Only life is brief;
Tears only wear the heart away.

56

My heart cries, Where is she? My heart must find
The answer, but my mind
Harries my heart back hard against the fact,
The brute accomplished act
Of death that love and hope cannot gainsay
And had no power to stay.
Then I feel that she struggled with life's pain
And death's despair in vain.

If I could know that she I love lives on,
That she is only gone
Upon a journey like a traveler,
If I had news of her,
Her loss would be less bitter to endure.
But nothing here is sure
And on the other side of death what lies
Must always be surmise.
No messenger has come to me and said,
"I spoke with your dear dead."
Yet though at times I doubt, at times I feel
A still influence steal

Across my heart as from the deep to tell
My heart that all is well,
Too tenuous a feeling to be caught
In shape or sound or thought;
Words cannot tell of it and if they could
Would not be understood.

Life's deepest meanings, dearest truths are those
That words cannot disclose.
How gross is he whose vision never wings
Beyond tangible things,
Who has no subtler values than a word
Can hold, who has not heard
Love's silence plainer than the thunder roll
When soul communes with soul.

Love's logic is obscure, yet truer than
The wisdom one can scan
In syllogisms. I cannot tell why
I loved, if I should try
No one would understand—lovers have such
Frail reasons, a mere touch
Is love's sufficiency and can contain
All ecstasy or pain.

So is it now with faith. The passing small
Events, words, feelings, all
The oracles I hear my wife speak through
Might be but mute to you,
But I catch even from the deep of death
Her still small voice of faith.

And to me even pain and death make sense,
The soul's magnificence
Shining more gloriously through the fire,
Deathlessly soaring higher,
Tried by its agony and made complete,
Victorious in defeat.

Seeing how much of courage and what love
A heart is capable of,
That being overwhelmed can stand and trust,
Shall I believe us dust?
How can I doubt that man is God or near it,
Having beheld her spirit?
So faith, like a fair wind from a far shore,
Comes sometimes unlooked-for,
And then the doubts that turn in my mind's mill
Grow quiet. I am still.

57

I cannot bear the thought that I
Am never against your heart to lie
Again, against your heart to find
Haven for heart and limbs and mind.
I have to believe that we will meet
Sometime somewhere on eternity street,
Or heaven would be only hell.

To lie by your side and feel the swell
Of your breast, the warmth of your hand, the
    touch
Of your lips! In the lonely night I clutch
At the hope I could not live without.
Damn the whispering devils of doubt!

Because a man must be a man
I shall go on as best I can
And do what comes to me to do,
But what I want is you, is you!

58

Forever has the saddest sound
Of any word I know:
It is the far-off places
Where I shall never go.

It is the places I have been
And cannot come again;
It is the last breath of my love—
Forever started then.

59

Full of loved things, my rooms have grown to be
An island of familiarity;
Katherine is gone, yet Katherine lives here still.
Everything in my rooms cries, Katherine! till
Sometimes I think I cannot stand to stay
Here longer, yet I cannot go away;
Here are the worn, dear things that I love best.
Yet it is here that I am loneliest,
Surrounded by the things that are my own.
For everything that now is mine alone
Is something that was also hers, and it
Cries always—desolate, desolate, desolate!
Turning my rooms into an echoing
Emptiness in my mind, where everything
Has power to bring her back, but not to life.
With everything I touch, I touch my wife!

60

Sorrow is such a friend of mine
I need not ask her in;
She slips in as the shadow
Of gladness that has been.

An uninvited visitor,
She sits at home with me.
I only wish that sorrow
Had joy's inconstancy.

61

Now in the evening when I come
Home to my empty house, still some
Sense in me cries that she is there,
That I shall see her on the stair,
That she will answer if I knock.
I turn the door key in the lock
And pause a moment listening for
Her footsteps, which will come no more.

How shall I drive it through my head
That she I love is really dead
And there will be when I come in
No one to say, "Where have you been?"

62

It is not only with my mind
I miss my wife, I think the blind
Must agonize like this for light,
Knowing they have no hope of sight.

I know that I have no hope of her,
But still I miss her, crave her, love her,
And with my flesh as much as brain
Thirst, cry for her, and feel the pain.

63

Always when Katherine and I went
Out for a drive, I held her hand;
Feeling her near, I was content;
Our clasped hands were a bridge that spanned
All loneliness. Sometimes we rode
For hours and no word passed our lips;
Deeper than speech love's silence flowed
Between our outstretched fingertips.

Now sometimes when by night I drive
On roads we used to take, I will
Forget that she is not alive
Beside me and forgetting still
Reach for the hand I cannot take,
Reach out, reach out until I ache.

Part Eight

*L*ove Is Strong
as Death

Christmas: A Step Back Toward Life

When I woke on that first Christmas morning of aloneness, I did not want to get out of bed. I had planned to be away on Christmas and had taken a trip to California, with the thought that I might stay there, but I had soon realized I was more alone in California than I was here in Missouri—living in my familiar apartment, doing my familiar work, meeting my familiar friends—so I had to come back.

I did not want to wake at all; if I could have slept through that Christmas, I believe I would have done so. But wake I did, and at my usual early hour; it was not even daylight yet.

As a child, I had learned to be an early riser. My grandfather had taught me that.

My grandfather had taught me many things. When I was a small boy, he and I would always be up hours before dawn, down in the kitchen, lighting the coal stove, where he would fix us heaping plates of potatoes and eggs. And on Christmas morning I would come creeping through the dark from my room into his. While he went downstairs "to see if Santa Claus has gotten here," I would lie impatiently in his huge feather bed; or more likely, I would leap up and down in its voluptuous billows, my mind a torrent and torment of imagination, and my body, often literally, at a fever pitch of anticipation, as I waited to hear his voice: "All right, Jim, you can come down. I believe Santa Claus has been here." Then I would make a headlong plunge down the stairs into the parlor.

My grandfather had taught me to read and write long before I had started to school. He had taught me out of fairytale books and history books, out of the Bible and books of poems. He loved Poe, so he cajoled and bribed me into memorizing "Annabel Lee," which I would recite for his friends for a penny.

As I lay there that Christmas morning, I wondered if that had been prophetic.

But lying in bed thinking back to earlier and happier Christmases was not going to help me to live through this one. My childhood and my grandfather were gone many years before.

And so was my wife—Katherine had died three months before.

Lying here thinking would not bring her back. All my thoughts—and all my prayers!—had not kept her alive.

I could not comprehend how such a thing could happen. Why should she have died? She must have asked why too, in the silence of her own soul, where none could hear her cry. But one thing she had showed me clearly, as I had kept watch beside her and shared her pain: Through prayer and faith and love, you can come to a place in your soul where the most that life can do to you is make you say, "Ouch!" and eventually it cannot even do *that*.

I still cannot understand how Love—and if there is a God, He *must* be Love—can make a world with so much pain and death; probably I never will. Half the things I have written have been my search for answers. I am sure my poems are part of my search.

How can I convey to you what, perhaps, the mind has no power to reach? What is the secret, silent wisdom of the heart? I only know that it is possible to catch a glimpse of things, not as we ordinarily experience them, but in another dimension—as from eternity?—and, in this larger frame, see that it is possible to have faith. Even when all visible support for faith is swept away, life and its events, however puzzling they may now seem to be, make sense and have meaning, and that meaning is good.

But I have gotten away from my story. I had to get out of bed and get through a day I dreaded to meet, Christmas without the one I love.

Christmas had meant so much to both of us. I remembered our first Christmas—before we were married; we had been going together about a year. The day I came to work in Silent Unity, we had started going together. She stopped me on that first day as I came through the office and told me that a group of fellows and girls were going to spend the weekend together. The fellows had rented one cottage, and the girls had rented another. Would I like to go? She had a car and would be glad to take me. By the time we went back to work on Monday, we were in love.

I pushed away the pillow that lay alongside me. Since she had died, I had slept with an extra pillow. I told myself it was to help me go to sleep, but I knew the pillow was more than that: for fourteen years I had slept beside my wife.

Slowly I swung my legs over the side of the bed and sat there in the dark. I was glad it was dark. In the dark, I could not see how empty the room was.

The clock in the hall struck the hour. I counted the

chimes: one, two, three, four, five, six. I loved that chiming clock; when I woke in the dark alone and heard it ringing out the hour, it gave me a sense of my whereabouts. It was a beautiful old banjo clock. Katherine and I had anguished over buying it, whether we could spend that much money.

I was glad we had; I needed things like the clock that helped me to locate myself at the center of myself. That was why I had not moved out of the house our apartment was in. When she died, my first thought was to run away, the house was so full of her.

I could not come into a room without her being in the room too. I could not sit in a chair without becoming aware that the empty chair beside me was hers. Wherever I turned, there was something that was hers, something that was ours like the clock, except that now there was no ours, there was only mine.

The apartment, its familiar rooms and objects, was a stabilizing element in my life. Here I was at home. This was a central location not only on the street but also in my soul.

We had lived here four years. We had had a hard time finding this apartment. The war was still on when we had moved in. Before we found it, we had lived in one room in a hotel with paper-thin walls and with neighbors who came home at three in the morning and battled. Only you who lived through the war and know how hard it was to find a decent place to live can appreciate how much that apartment meant to us. It was on the second floor of an old apartment house with only four beautifully spacious apartments in it. It even had a screened-in porch and a pantry. It had a front hall and fireplace in the living room. Not a fireplace where you could burn wood; it had a radiant gas burner with a crinkly asbestos sheet in it but the flames ran sparkling across it, and when we lay in front of it, it spread its warmth through our bodies and glowed in our minds almost as much as a log fire would have. At least it was not hard for us to convince ourselves that this was so. We had loved to lie in front of it. We had a big wool serape we bought in Mexico on a vacation trip, and we would lie on that.

But I was not in Mexico, I was at home, and I probed with my feet until I found my slippers.

I walked into the living room and lit the fireplace. For several minutes I stood in front of it, watching the sparkling flames, letting the heat slowly soak into my face and hands. The heat had not started yet in the radiators.

I had left a record of Christmas carols on the record player, but I did not turn it on. I decided that I was probably the only one awake in the building, and I did not want to waken the others. "They are the lucky ones," I thought. "Let them sleep."

I wanted to open the presents that were under the tree, but also I didn't want to. As long as I could put off opening them, I would have something to look forward to. I had a good idea what might be in them, that is, all except one.

There was a gift that was a puzzlement. It was a large box. Three days before Christmas, Katherine's best friend—my friend too, for we had worked together many years—had brought the box. "You are to take this home," she had told me, "and put it under the tree and not open it until Christmas morning."

"I've bought a tree, but I haven't put it up yet," I said. "You think I ought to?"

"Yes, I do," she said "If Katherine were here, that's what she'd want you to do, isn't that so?"

"She's not here," I said. "Maybe I'd be better off if I forgot it was Christmas."

"You can't forget it's Christmas. Christmas always meant too much to Katherine and you. That's why I think you ought to put up your tree and open your presents Christmas morning, just as you always have. And I want you to promise you'll open this gift last of all."

"Why?" I said. "What's in it?"

"If I told you that, it wouldn't be a Christmas present. But yes, I will tell you what's in it. The spirit of Christmas is in it. That's why I want you to open it last. It will carry you triumphantly through the day."

I was glad that she asked me to put up the tree and open my presents Christmas morning, because I wanted to do it. Although I was frightened of what this Christmas would bring, I still wanted Christmas to be Christmas.

Katherine and I had always made a big thing of Christmas and the Christmas tree. We even had decorations that my mother had given me, remnants of my childhood. Trimming a tree and rising on Christmas morning to open presents under it seemed almost a rule of life that I could not violate. I suppose it is foolish to build patterns like this into your life, but most of us do.

I went into the kitchen and fixed myself a cup of coffee. That took awhile. I am not a cook. My mother was a good cook, and so was my wife. When she became too ill to cook, I had tried feebly to learn, but as long as she could get to the stove, my wife had insisted on cooking for us.

I sat at the kitchen table and slowly drank my coffee. When I finished, I poured another cup and carried it into the dining room.

I had set the Christmas tree on a table in a corner of the dining room. It was not a big tree. I thought as I stood there that it had been foolish of me to decorate it. I turned on the lights on the tree. It was pretty, I thought, and sat for a time staring at it and sipping my coffee. Slowly I became aware that the light was returning to the world outside my window. I walked to the window and looked up and down the street. It was a cloudless sky. It would be clear and cold, I decided. Everything—the leafless trees, the empty yards, the sleeping houses—looked gray and bare in the half light of early morning.

Slowly I opened the presents. I do not remember now what they were. I am sure there was one from my mother; she usually sent me something handmade. And I am sure there was one from a friend named Mark. I was going to have Christmas dinner with him. He had had multiple sclerosis for eight years, and I had become his best friend, at times his only friend; his wife had left him.

I believe there were some other presents, but at last there remained only the box my friend had brought me with instructions that it must be the last gift to open. As I said, it was a puzzlement. I could not guess what she might be giving to me or even why she had exchanged gifts with my wife but never with me.

The box was neatly wrapped in Christmas paper and had a large bow on it. I have always envied people who can tie bows. When I make them, they turn out to look like blackbirds' nests. I tore off the wrapping and opened the box.

There were three packages in it, all carefully wrapped in silver metallic paper bound in a red bow. It struck me that this had been the way Katherine wrapped her gifts to me. I lifted them out and placed them on the floor. They felt like books. I picked up the first one. There was a small envelope attached to it. On it were a few handwritten words. For an incomprehensible moment, I stared at the handwriting.

I knew that my friend's handwriting resembled Katherine's. But was my friend, or was my mind, playing a strange trick on me? I read the words:

> *"To a poet with all my love.*
> *From Katherine"*

I tore open the package. In it was the Cambridge edition of Tennyson's poems. Almost instantly I realized that someone was giving me this because they wanted me to read "In Memoriam," the poem that Tennyson labored and agonized over for seventeen years as he searched for faith after the death of his young friend, Arthur Henry Hallam.

Later my friend told me that Katherine had told her how we had seen a replica first edition of "In Memoriam" in a shop that dealt in rare and old books, but when she went to buy it, the book had been sold, and this was the only volume she could find with the complete "In Memoriam" in it.

But I did not stop to think about the book and the poem now. I did not stop to think. I reached for the next package. With trembling hands, I plucked the little card pasted to its top. On it was drawn a small red heart with an arrow through it. I read the card:

> *"I always wanted you to read this. Love, Katherine."*

For a moment I could not believe what I was reading. I tore open the package. The book was Thomas Mann's *Joseph and His Brothers*. It had just been published that year, but it was not a new book; it was a collection of four of his earlier novels that had been published separately. They were *The Tales of Jacob, Young Joseph, Joseph in Egypt,* and *Joseph the Provider.* Katherine was a constant reader. She had read these novels one by one and told me how much she liked them. But why, out of the myriad books she had read, had she chosen these stories?

At that moment I was incapable of coherent thought, but I have often thought about it since. Was it the story of Jacob and Rachel, which ends with Rachel's death, that she wanted me to read? Her wanting me to read the stories was not, however, a dying thought; long before she had become ill, she had urged me to read them. Did she know, in the strange way we sometimes have of knowing without knowing, that she would be the Rachel to my Jacob? I have often wondered about that. Life is not at all what it mostly seems to be; we are impelled along our outward course by silent inward forces; many things go on in the depths of our souls that never rise to shallow enough levels of our minds for us to catch them with our conscious thinking.

I reached for the third package. There was no card pasted on this. By now I was down on my knees, my hands shaking so hard that I could hardly direct them. With a mighty effort, I tore the paper off the package. Somehow I had expected it to be another book. But it was not a book. It was a red leather box. I opened the box.

Inside the box there was a narrow shelf on which lay an envelope with two words penciled on it: *"To Jim."*

I lifted out the shelf. In the box were twelve golf balls.

Carefully I took out of the envelope a handwritten letter. There was no question now, this was Katherine's handwriting, these were Katherine's words. As my eyes and my heart stormed through the penciled sentences, I knew that this was Katherine's heart I held in my hands.

My Beloved,

Steady, Jim, steady, dear heart. When you read this, you have survived til Christmas, and the worst is over now.

You and I have dreamed dreams and thought thoughts and been, oh, so close, my dearest. If your heart cannot find the answer to "why, why, why," then for the time being please accept my sure faith and firm trust that all is well with me. For you these may yet be aching hours, and I have felt for you and been greatly concerned, but I have been comforted in this thought: Surely in surrendering you to the law of Love, I have also surrendered you to greater growth, greater understanding, and yes, I am sure, to happiness and joy and fulfillment. Remember to tell me that was so, My Golden One! Never refuse happiness and look with approval and blessing upon it.

You know the way now to the Dwelling of Light, and I am glad, and if ever you are fearful look out in the sky while I no doubt shall be a little Star, how burning bright shall I be in my love for you! I shall keep busy doing my work, waiting until we are together again.

You keep busy with your work, too. V.V.V. You are always in my heart.

Because I have known with you love and passion, and because you brought me beauty and richness in thought and perception of mind and spirit, and because we have watched together firelight and candlelight and sunlight and moonlight, I count myself the most fortunate of women.

I shall bless thee now, and thou shalt forever be a Blessing.

Eternally, in understanding and in Perfect Love,
Your Katherine
Steady, Jim, steady, dear heart, the worst is over
now.

I do not know how I managed to read it through, and I will never be sure what happened during those next few minutes.

All I remember now is that when I came to myself, I was stretched out on the floor, and I was weeping as I have never wept before or since. A flood, a storm of sobs was bursting from me, convulsing every inch of my body. I was pounding my chest with my fists. I may have been pounding my head against the floor. My body ached.

But when I stood up and stumbled to the bathroom and washed my face, I suddenly realized, to my astonishment, that my mind was clear and my heart was light.

I have often wondered if it was not the accumulated energy that for many months I had had to gather and hold in, so that I might show the calm spirit I felt I had to show, that must have come cascading out of me in such tumultuous fashion. I do not know whether it was more an expression of anguish or rejoicing, they were so entangled. Undoubtedly it was my wild grief at the loss of my wife and my pent-up rage at life and death. But also it was an outpouring of joy in my love for her and her love for me, and sudden overwhelming sense of our undying oneness.

Emotions that run too deep may never reach the surface. Now these Christmas gifts from my wife had opened all the secret gates and sluices of my inmost being.

I was drained, but I was filled with an extraordinary sense of release. I was free.

The storm had passed.

I rose from the floor, I took a bath, I dressed in my best suit and happiest tie, I went out to breakfast and to meet the day.

I ate dinner that day with Mark. After dinner he beat me twice at chess, which made his Christmas a happy one—happier, at least, than it might have been—and that made *my* Christmas happier too.

It was late when I got home, late enough for bed. I had left the gifts under the tree. Now I picked them up and looked at them again—the golf balls, *In Memoriam*, *Joseph and His Brothers*. I noticed that *Joseph and His Brothers* had 1207 pages; I would not read it tonight. But I scanned the last page, where Joseph tells his brothers that they are all in a play, God's play, and that it is time to forget about all the ills which had occurred—God had turned it to good. I read his concluding words: "It is the future we are interested in. Sleep in peace. Tomorrow in God's good providence we shall take our way back into that quaint and comic land of Egypt."

That seemed a right thought to end the day with, and I was *ready* to end it. I was tired; I had never felt *more* tired. I hardly lay down in bed before I was asleep.

The next morning was a workday again. I arose at the usual time, in the usual way, and went to work.

64

A year exactly after Katherine died
I dreamed of her. I was alone inside
A huge hall, and I wept with wild despair
When something made me look behind me. There
My wife was, and she laid my head upon
Her breast and kissed me till my tears were gone;
I lay close to her heart. Then something broke
The thread, the dream dissolved, and I awoke.

For a long moment I lay at the black
Threshold of mind while consciousness crept back,
And slowly I became aware that I
Was not alone. Someone was standing by
My bed, half leaning over me. I felt
A start of terror, then felt terror melt,
For on my cheek came the remembered touch
Of Katherine's lips, dear lips I loved so much.

Her kiss was like a blessing, like a grace.
I tried to turn and look into her face
But when I tried, it seemed as if it took

Forever to find strength to turn and look,
And with my first faint movement she was gone.
You may think that I was but dreaming on,
Dreaming I was awake—so it may be—
But I shall always know that it was she.

65

When she was living, often I would be
Writing at night, and she
Would go into another room to sleep.
I would work on, a deep
Contentment filling me, a sense serene,
Although she was unseen.

Now sometimes as I write there comes again
That same deep peace as then.
It comes from nothing that I see or hear,
Only I feel her near
And loving me. Then I work on without
Even the will to doubt.

When I am worn out and my work is through
And I must go into
The other room, I shall go without dread.
I shall but go to bed
Yet one time more—as it was in my life—
And sleep beside my wife.

66

Anything less than utter trust in life
And love would be like treason to my wife.
Because of what she was, even the pain
Was not all loss, something in it was gain;
I come forth stronger than I was, not sad
But with a faith I never knew I had,
The faith that life is good, the strength to press
After a meaning in the meaningless,
The wisdom to submerge the fraction of
Myself in the vast integer of love.

Life is a strong urge. It cannot stand still
But must go forward, and there is a will
To live in me, a love of life. To me
If there were nothing in eternity
Save life's brief bubble, no immortal soul,
No hope beyond the grave, no God, no goal,
And we were but the children of mischance,
The universe would have significance
Because we are and draw this life-stuff, breath!
One moment's life outweighs the whole of death.

Love Is Strong as Death

I have no reach of thought to comprehend
The meaning of our life or see the end
We serve, but know our limits are not birth
And death, the three dimensions of this earth.
I have a sense but dimly understood
But still a sense of being used for good;
Life's meaning is as far beyond all seeming
As we must be beyond our own cells' dreaming
And what power can they have to understand
What speech is or the motion of a hand?

Yet more is to be found in us to meet
Whatever comes, though it may be defeat;
Though we may fall, we do not fall alone,
But share a meaning larger than our own;
We are one with the all; our small selves merge
Into the living will, the upward urge
That rises from unfathomable springs
Of being, the compassion for all things
That live and feel and suffer; we are part
Of one vast action, pulses in one heart.

How shall we count the battle won or lost
Or meter out the gain or weigh the cost?
Life has a meaning measured not by length
Or even by our weakness or our strength;
Not only by bright triumphs and full years
May life be measured, but sometimes by tears.
It is the living, life is measured by;
The aim of life is living. She and I
Shared thought and love and passion, watched
    the light
Together and together faced the night.

I was her husband and she was my wife;
Life gave itself to us who gave ourselves to life.

67

I have lived many lives. Now one is ended,
And time cannot turn back upon its track.
I think my sorrow never will be mended
But sorrowing and wishing will not bring her back.

Deep in my heart I feel that she will never
Be far from me, love cannot lose its own;
But now I wave farewell across forever
And turn and look toward life where I must walk
    alone.

Time takes too long to travel empty-hearted,
And where my road may wind I do not know;
The journey is uncertain and uncharted.
Now I will grieve no longer—it is time to go.

Love's Rose

Love has less substance than a lover's breath
Heaved in a sigh and spun into a song,
And yet it has a power to outlast death;
Heaven and earth will not endure as long.
After the fiery twilight of the gods,
When all our demons and our deities
Perish together and cast down their rods
And crowns, love will rise weeping from its knees
And raise a world beyond the reach of doom,
That will survive even our unbelief,
That will not wither with the withering bloom
Of time or fade with life's fast-fading leaf,
But like a delicate and deathless rose
Will blossom and burn red in winter snows.

About James and Katherine Freeman

Born in Wilmington, Delaware, in 1912, James Dillet Freeman moved to Kansas City with his family when he was ten years old. He attended Kansas City public schools and the University of Missouri, where he majored in English and was graduated with honors in 1932. He began writing verse at the age of ten, and by the time he finished college, his poems had been published in national publications.

While still in college, Jim was given summer work in 1929 at Unity School of Christianity by invitation of Unity's cofounder, Myrtle Fillmore. After a year of postgraduate work at the University, he rejoined the Unity staff in 1933, serving in the School's Silent Unity prayer ministry as a letter writer.

Young Lucy Katherine Veronica Gilwee came to work for Unity School in the 1920s right out of high school. Born in 1908 of an Irish father and an Italian mother and raised in the Irish-Catholic tradition, she was one of five children. One of her brothers, Bill Gilwee, also worked at Unity School and later became a Jackson County prosecutor in the 1930s. Her parents had immigrated to America and, as happened to so many immigrants, the family name Kilkee came through the immigration process as Gilwee.

Though small in stature—Katherine was only 5 feet tall—she was an untiring Silent Unity worker, eventually becoming the immediate assistant of longtime Silent Unity director May Rowland. Jim Freeman recalls how they met:

"When I went to work in Silent Unity in 1933, I did not want to work for a religion and I did not intend to stay. But on the very first day, this pretty girl came up to me and told me that a group of boys who worked there and a group of girls who also worked there were going to spend the weekend at Unity Farm (now Unity Village). The boys had rented one cabin on the picnic grounds and the girls another. She was sure the fellows would be happy to have me move in with them to help pay the rent. She owned a car, and she would be happy to take me. That was in July. We rented the cabins every weekend that summer. On October 26 of the next year, Katherine and I were married."

Together the Freemans worked in Silent Unity through the 1930s and into the early war years. Occasionally, Jim was asked to go on speaking trips to Unity centers across the country and Katherine would accompany him. By 1943 Jim had written pamphlets for Unity and was writing poetry for *Daily Word,* Unity's daily devotional magazine.

In 1945 Unity was experiencing the need for trained ministers, and Jim was led to organize the training program that today is Unity School for Religious Studies. He continued to serve as director of Unity's ministerial program in Silent Unity until 1965. He received ordination as a Unity minister in 1967. Over a short period of time after Katherine's illness and death in 1948, Jim wrote most of the poems found in this book. The poems remained in his private collection until now.

In 1971 Jim succeeded May Rowland as director of the Silent Unity worldwide prayer ministry. Shortly afterward, he became a member of the board of trustees and first vice president of Unity School. In 1984 Jim retired from these positions in order to devote more time to writing and speaking on behalf of the Unity movement.

However, it is as an author that James Dillet Freeman is best known. He has inspired literally millions. He has been called "a modern-day transcendentalist" who writes in the tradition of Emerson, Thoreau, and Whitman. His work has been translated into thirteen languages, and he has been published in *The New Yorker, Saturday Review, Scientific Monthly, Christian Herald, New York Times, Reader's Digest,* and many other publications. For many years, Jim has written a monthly column, "Life Is a Wonder," for *Unity Magazine,* and his poems appear regularly in *Daily Word.*

Jim Freeman's widest acclaim comes as a poet. It is estimated that published copies of his poems exceed 500 million. His work has been taken to the moon twice, a distinction he shares with no other author. His 1941 "Prayer for Protection" was taken aboard Apollo 11 in July 1969 by Lunar Module pilot Edwin E. Aldrin, Jr. Aldrin had the poem with him when he made his historic moonwalk. Two years later Jim's 1947 poem "I Am There," which is in this volume, went to the moon with Colonel James B. Irwin on Apollo 15. Irwin left a microfilm copy of the poem on the moon!

In 1995 "I Am There" was featured on the television program "Angels II: Beyond the Light" on NBC. In talking about the poem, which is probably his best-known work, Jim says: "Of all the things I have ever written, 'I Am There' has meant the most to the most people. I wrote it in great anguish of spirit, out of a deep personal need. It has been reprinted many times and people have written from all over the world to tell me how much it has meant to them."

Jim has published twelve books, some by Doubleday, Harper & Row, and some by Unity Books, including *The Hilltop Heart, The Story of Unity, The Case for Reincarnation,* and *Once Upon a Christmas.* He also contributed a chapter in the Unity anthology *New Thought for a New Millennium.*

After all these years and accomplishments, a quiet tribute to Katherine remains in Jim's published works. During the 1940s, two Freeman poems would sometimes be selected for an issue of *Daily Word.* Using his wife's original family name, Jim insisted on giving the authorship of the extra poem to the young woman who shared her life and love with him—Katherine Kilkee.

Printed in the U.S.A.   48-1231-7.5M-12-99